Mother, Loose

Mother, Loose

Poems by
Brandel France de Bravo

Accents Publishing • Lexington, Kentucky • 2015

Copyright © 2015 by Brandel France de Bravo
All rights reserved

Printed in the United States of America

Accents Publishing
Editor: Katerina Stoykova-Klemer
Cover Image: iStockphoto.com/JoeKlune
Cover Design: Simeon Kondev

ISBN: 978-1-936628-28-5
First Edition

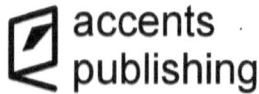

Accents Publishing is an independent press for brilliant voices. For a catalog of current and upcoming titles, please visit us on the Web at

www.accents-publishing.com

Contents

Foreword / ix

The Old Woman in the Shoe / 1
Grammar School / 3
In Transit / 5
A Perfect Sacrifice (still it lingered near) / 6
The Night Kitchen / 7
Ladybird Ladybird Fly Away Home Your House Is on Fire / 8
The Queen of Hearts / 9
Returns & Exchanges / 10
Jack Sprat / 11
Dialogue with the Body / 12
Husband Peter / 15
Mother, Tongue / 16
I Regret to Inform You / 17
Per Capita / 18
An Egg's Tale / 22
As After a Sleep / 24
Taking a Bow / 25
In the Arms of Morpheus I / 26
Pussy's in the Well / 27
In the Arms of Morpheus II / 28
In the Arms of Morpheus III / 29
Four and Twenty Blackbirds / 30
Merry-Go-Round / 31

About the Author / 33

Acknowledgments / 35

Foreword

It was a great honor to read Brandel France de Bravo's *Mother, Loose* and to select it for the winner of the Accents Publishing chapbook contest. As I moved through this bold, vibrant, and compelling chapbook, it became increasingly apparent that I was in the company of a writer who understands the difficulty of capturing the ineffable in language, and yet with great care and craft, grappled this unwieldy medium into astute and arresting poems. These jewel-like poems—both in their precision and beauty—are as dazzling and intelligent as they are entrancing and enthralling.

I was struck time and again by how France de Bravo transports the reader from familiar to utterly unexpected contexts through startling imaginative leaps and unexpected metaphors. She reminds the reader of the power and pleasure of metaphor and of our understanding and experience of how metaphor deepens and transforms what lies on both sides of the metaphorical equation. For example, in "A Perfect Sacrifice (still it lingers near)," Mary, of the familiar nursery rhyme, and her little lamb are recast in Nail-Like-Gnu where "the Vietnamese lady pumiced Mary's heels and snipped at the lamb's cuticles." Later, Mary exchanges her plaid kilt and navy sweater for the lamb's pelt, Mary is metaphorically reclothed in a desire "spreading to every part of her." When the fleece slips from Mary's shoulders, the terrible and beautiful way that desire drives us is revealed when Mary touches her mouth, "saliva gathering at the corners. It was a maw."

The textured meanings of maw recur again in the poem "Jack Sprat." The speaker faced with "sinew and glisten" navigates the subtle but considerable distinction between the hunger of desire and its darker guise, gluttony:

> She licked his arm clean.
> He licked her vanity.
> One day, in the pantry,

> their tongues met
> and they knew salty-sweet,
> felt time running in place.
> Afterwards, Jack lit a cigarette.
>
> The rest is a blur, like glass
> smeared with butter.
> Jack remembers fetching his pail.
> He remembers the whoosh and flash,
> spitting heat, and his mother's words.
> *Never throw water on a grease fire.*

Throughout the book, France de Bravo uses familiar nursery rhymes and tales both as a canvas for her own imagination and inventiveness, and also to create a lens through which other poems can be read. This creates a cumulative effect that reveals a spectrum of tones of registers that allow the poems singularly and collectively to open into unexpected and compelling places.

Many of the poems in *Mother, Loose* grapple with the universal, yet profoundly solitary experience of grief. Across several poems we witness the speaker struggle to observe and comprehend a mother's descent into absence. The poems that chronicle this journey are forceful and heartbreaking, and most powerful among these are the Morpheus poems ("In the Arms of Morpheus" I, II and III). In "In the Arms of Morpheus I" through the mother's slow collapse, the speaker conveys the fragility of language and the helplessness of witnessing:

> She rises from the commode,
> pull-ups at her ankles, then dizzy,
> falls forward, forearms, palms
> on the bed. She shakes her head,
> sighs *singerie,* French for monkey
> business. She doesn't want ....

In the last stanza, the reader can sense the need for precision as surrogate for those moments in grief when expansiveness is impossible:

        mannered   irreverent
        neither erect   nor on all fours
        corseted   extruding

Throughout the collection, one also recognizes the urgency to move forward, to speak the unsayable, to transform pain into beauty. France de Bravo acknowledges that "there's a fist in poignant" ("Into the Arms of Morpheus II"), but bravely, and with great care and skill, and despite the pain, she delivers poems of hope and renewal.

Patty Paine
Judge for the 2014 Accents Publishing Chapbook Contest

"Old woman, old woman, old woman," quoth I
"O whither, O whither, O whither, so high?"
"To brush the cobwebs off the sky!"
"Shall I go with thee?" "Aye, by and by."

—Mother Goose rhyme

Mother, you are the one mouth
I would be a tongue to.

—Sylvia Plath, "Poem for a Birthday"

The Old Woman in the Shoe

Moored in bramble but still I tell them "row."
What else can I do with these charges,
bothersome as bunions? In the dark of the hull,

their sequin-sweat catches light, and they turn
orphaned faces toward it, gulping air
from the open portholes. I removed the laces

after Dimple Dan died, hid them below deck.
Oar-breath and the clatter of shackles keep time,
as one by one the children fold, forehead to knees.

Singing softly, I carry the weary to the bow
where five cots wait and pitch the dead
into the toss and roil of thorn. Life is a tight fit.

For dinner I give them broth, shouting,
"Cup your hands. Them that's got the will
knows not to mind the scald." What does not leak

is lapped, but the bread is mine. I eat the crust,
throw away the rest for all to see, and search
the horizon with my glass, squint for delivery.

Hear *my* lullaby: someday, the anchor will lift.
This cargo a memory, I will let my sails out,
pull them taut as I see fit. Captain of my shoe,

my tongue will take me where I want to go.

Grammar School

America the Beautiful was our soundtrack, each
    of the twenty-four frames per second as bottomless,
open as the holes in our desks where the ink bottles
    weren't, like the cloakroom without cloaks—
just parkas and yellow raincoats. Hands perpetually
    raised, the smell of mimeographs redolent
as our mothers' perfume, violet fingers quivering
    in the air. *God shed your grace on me,*
which would be the lavatory key, shackled to a wood
    brick bigger than a 7-year-old's hand, thighs,
buttocks clenched against shame. And naps
    at our amber waving desks on pillows of crossed
arms, *my soul to keep,* as the radiators, skeletal
    beneath the windows, sang their hiss-and-clang
lullaby. Waking, we tied on our thinking caps,
    index fingers ready to march once more
across the *Weekly Reader,* to bushwhack through
    the dense green words,
                              fearful of ambush.

America the Beautiful was our soundtrack, each
    of us a majestic purple note, and each of the twenty-four
frames a forspacious story, until the projector,
    its young eaten, stutters to white, until
Mrs. Boston, roaming the aisles, would single out
    the one not seated to teach us proper
speech. "Where's Antony?" she'd ask, or "Where's
    Jerome?" and Denise, Deborah and "T," falling
like straight men, hang men every time
    would point to the student clapping erasers or standing
startled at the pencil sharpener, and shout, proud
    to know the answer to something, "There he go!"
And Mrs. Boston, hands on hips, would turn to us,
    smirking slightly and using the double negative

I found so thrilling—my white mother would have
     slapped me for it—to correct: "I don't see him
going nowhere. There he *is*," she scolded.
     I knew the difference between the two verbs,
but the lesson came too late for me,
     going always a substitute for being in a life
spent leaving: this classroom, this
     brotherhood, this sea to shining, and Antony
          still not nowhere.

In Transit

> No one expected me. Everything awaited me.
>
> —Patti Smith, *Just Kids*

After Kansas and before the bony ground, that tubular
nowhere of suspended belief, between always winter
and the spare room (even coat sleeves must malinger),

or an empty stairwell you enter from any floor, the door
locking behind you, multiple beginnings with only one
end but it's your choice when to exit to the sun-sodden

sidewalk, not just a through but a *there*, or circumstances
that free as they frustrate, minor deaths which resurrect,
a canceled meeting, snow day, power out, missed flight,

idling between those left behind and those who await,
welcome to this holiday express in a city that never was
a destination, let the doctor's to-do footsteps stay

in the corridor today, let the magazine pages inside
stop turning, your dressing gown fall open: it is time
for your examination, this is the hare moment the hounds

raced past, the tiny gift buried in packing peanuts,
fly away, spongy as what-if, it is the lily no one planted,
unexpected as a teenage girl's gorgeous yellow rage.

A Perfect Sacrifice (still it lingered near)

Spring had come and the pear trees, sheared of their white blossoms, were flaunting new green skin. Mary decided to skip school. She called the lamb and told her to meet at Nails-like-Gnu. The Vietnamese lady pumiced Mary's heels and snipped at the lamb's cuticles. Mary and the lamb picked "Teat Peach" polish and flip-flopped out the door, cotton puffs between their toes. The security guard at Victoria's Secret said lambs were not allowed so Mary went in alone. She came out a few minutes later carrying a big pink shopping bag, two thongs inside. At the Food Court they got diet sodas and headed to Mary's house because her parents were at work. "Let's try on each other's clothes," said Mary. "Awesome," said the lamb. Mary wrapped herself in the lamb's fleece. "God, it's *so* warm." The lamb put on Mary's plaid kilt, navy sweater, and knee socks. "I'm gonna follow the rules now," the lamb giggled, giving a little salute. Mary looked at the lamb, and a current ran through her, more powerful than the sight of Nick's number pulsing on her cell phone. It was like the thread-pull between her legs whenever Nick's breath filled her ear. Only, the hollow feeling was in her stomach and spreading to every part of her. The fleece slid from Mary's shoulders. She touched her mouth, saliva gathering at the corners. It was a maw.

The Night Kitchen

It all began with a sleepless moon
counting cows and covering the counters
with sudsy light. The dented and rusty
still speak of that night, how *back in the day*
they used to dine with the dish and spoon,
and the young follow in their footsteps:
the trivet eloped with the teapot,
the spatula proposed to the pan,
and somewhere, they say,
the sieve and whisk are shacking up.

But the carving knife keeps company
with no one. Head buried deep
in a wooden block, he shuns the dull
familiar, this futile utensil love.
Let them tie their knots. He will write
mash notes to occlusive consonants,
the plosive "d" of *d*ivide, *d*ivorce
and … Sometimes at night
he can be heard moaning softly,
stirred by the glint of memory:

the firm grip of the farmer's wife,
the three tails writhing,
the mice who never saw what was coming.

Ladybird Ladybird Fly Away Home Your House Is on Fire

standing by the flowering white yucca between
Christmas and New Year's in a valley surrounded
by mountains like Chinese scroll paintings
phone in my hand standing in the garden of
a house I no longer live in my mother says
"x-ray" her dry cough flowering unremarkable
except for its constancy walking less the year before
a winded valley surrounded by mountains until
the smokeless fingers grew bulbs (they called it
"clubbing") sent smokeless signals "please"
I said "see someone" and after Christmas the
house I once lived in phoned the garden saying
"x-ray" like a painting "mass" white as yucca

The Queen of Hearts

This morning I left a tart freshly baked
steaming on the sill, and still it waits.
I have only this summer.
There will be no others.
Where is my knave with his knife
who dared to slice what was not his
and lick the sharp edge after?
Where is my conniver, my ravisher,
my thief? Jack of all mischief
worshipful as Black Mass.

In the Himalayas, I hear, heartless
in his robes, eating nothing that has eyes.
No, in Dearborn, driving canned food,
taking collection, never a coin
from the plate. No, in Des Moines
one basement day at a time
praising a power that is not mine.

All this abnegation—an abomination.
No one to trespass my kitchen,
desert with my desserts, just
a solitaire full sore eating
every one, the crumbs gathering
like sand between my breasts, the day's
mandala destroyed with undressing.
All that he has given up, I will gain
and carry where they may wonder
giving gravida to my grief.

My subjects say I let him break
the rules and now the ruler, broken.

Returns & Exchanges

I've been in and out of stores
shopping for a metaphor
but can't find what I'm looking for.
You say: My joints hurt.
I say: You need a new roof.
You say: I can't swallow.
I say: You're behind on your payments.
You say: I'm out of breath.
I say: the Bank wants it back.
You say: I can't feel my toes.
I say: Let's fill the john
with cement mix
and storm out to the applause
of the half-hinged screen door.
It turns out foreclosure
wasn't what I wanted.

The customer is always.
With a credit to my account
I'm driving on an eight-lane highway,
faster than the speed limit,
semis like linebackers on either side.
You say: My joints hurt.
I say: None of the stations are coming in.
You say: I can't swallow.
I say: Adjust the sun visor.
You say: I'm out of breath.
I say: look for a rest stop.
You say: I can't feel my toes.
I say: Something's trying to pass us.

We both can sense it
in the blind spot,
how it will overtake us.

Jack Sprat

He looked like six o' clock
and she the face.
Together they were bacon
—sinew and glisten—
and called a platter home.
She licked the welcome mat.
He licked the light switches.
She licked his arm chair.
He licked her vanity.
One day, in the pantry,
their tongues met
and they knew salty-sweet,
felt time running in place.
Afterwards, Jack lit a cigarette.

The rest is a blur, like glass
smeared with butter.
Jack remembers fetching his pail.
He remembers the whoosh and flash,
spitting heat, and his mother's words.
Never throw water on a grease fire.

Dialogue with the Body

I thought about leaving you.
But you didn't.

Why did you treat me so badly?
I was testing your love,
but those days are over.

I was a cigarette under your heel.
You inhaled—admit it.

If I said "stop," you heard "more."
I thought you enjoyed a little rough play.
Besides, who had who in bondage?

We used to have fun.
I still love you. I'm just not
in love with you.

Look me in the eye when you say that.
I don't trust mirrors anymore.

We're more like roommates now.
I'd like to scale down, move into
something with clean lines.

*I'm sick of you micromanaging me,
tired of 2 of these, 1 of those,
working my core.*
It's my way of saying sorry
I took you for granted.

Chocolates make a better apology.
You'll thank me one day.

*I wasn't as beautiful
as you made me out to be.*

Beauty is wasted
on the beautiful.

You don't take me anywhere.
You don't take me anywhere.

A body needs a body.
After all I've given you?
Sinewy, stubbled, bountiful,
smooth, man, woman.

You seem so distant
and happy without me.
You're no help
with Sudoku.

I can almost remember
the time before you:
the swaddling sea,
my neck a small boat.
Those hands are dead now.

Who will take care of me
when you're gone?
Proper arrangements
will be made, your care
entrusted to a stranger.

Where will you go?
I will be a passenger
on a highway that bends.
I'll ride through cropped hills,
cows still as mushrooms.

Can you hear me now?
You're all rhythm
and no melody.

Then sing with me.
Help me carry the tune.
Yes, I will be the words
in our little threnody.

Husband Peter

The roundness fools,
its moist interior feels
fecund at first.
I fear we're living
at the bottom of a dry well.
There he keeps me very,
feeding me seeds.
A life without seasons
bland as uncooked gourd.

The noon sun dangles over us,
a key out of reach.
I welcome the blaze
that turns our one room
into an eyelid.
Only then can I
pull my dreams
over me.

When the sun goes down
my husband dines by candlelight.
The smell of singed flesh
does not sicken him.
Our home grows tight
since the first quickening.
Who will be born here?

I scratch messages into the wall
but the letters
drop to the floor motionless
white worms
until our feet are buried,
my nails soft and useless.

He told me there was water.

Mother, Tongue

"Here," said the midwife guiding my hand,
and I caught, then brought the soft, slippery
weight, not covered in vernix but blood,
eye level. "It's a liver," I cried
before noticing my papoose's papillae.

I swaddled the slippery softness, my little
lingua, frankly feeling tender,
dare I say, iconic, golden
—Madonna, child, mother, tongue—
and cooing *gosse* like the one who
birthed me, French for baby goose.

I Regret to Inform You

I regret knowing, the way it changes
everything and nothing. I regret
cell death and its absence. I regret I *am*
the person you think I am. I regret
the days turned years waiting
and the luminous arriving
always eclipsed. I regret having
no sense of humor, feeling like Haiti
when I'm Liechtenstein, just as tiny but,
thanks for asking, fine. I regret
showing you what I am unable to see,
my wattled profile, baldly appraising gaze.
I regret leaving the back door open
and I regret closing it. I regret the odor
of obligation, being the small hair
that will not budge and the tongue
that must protest it. I regret
the tumor's intelligence, the way
it dodges the needle, pretends
to swallow poison. I regret this broken
mask and I regret your looking.
I regret waiting until now
to wait on you, not anointing your feet
with oil sooner. I regret the raspberries
I failed to feed you with a spoon.
I regret that after our meal
I will be left to clear the table.

Per Capita

> As I was going out one day,
> My head fell off and rolled away.
> But when I saw that it was gone,
> I picked it up and put it on.
>
> —Mother Goose rhyme
>
> In September 2006, gunmen opened the doors of the Sol y Sombra discotheque in Uruapan, in the western Mexican state of Michoacán, and threw five human heads onto the dance floor.
>
> —BBC news

1.

A remote Mexican village,
a cult, the rumored stash
of guns, the leader a defrocked
priest, the robes they made
even visiting women wear,
the halos of tin foil, the angel
who'd joined from the Philippines,
who told me how the devil
gets in, the priest's Roy Orbison
hair, *smaller than the smallest gnat,*
she said, the altar boys on either side.
He sits on the edge of your eyelid,
she whispered, the priest's
ringed hand I was told to kiss,
hides in the treetops of your lashes
until he sees an opening.

2.

The weary, maybe sick black
man in front of me, the blonde

with dark roots social-working
his ear, aural elbowing all of us
as we vibrate in our seats, wait
                      for the stop
where we'll escape like blood
this metal body that forces us to feel
the other's warm leg, waver between
the woman's voice and the man's eyelids,
as though there are only two pedals
                      on any bus.

3.

Pinocchio's, flue-ish
Cyrano's, Jewish
Aquiline, porcine
Fur-lined, gold mine
Roman, out of joint
Picked, fixed, pointy
In business sticky
"Pro," posey-crazy
Sachet-savvy, pug
Hoover, deviated
Ski-jump, one-bump,
Boxer's resume
Pierced, porous, hook
Always in a book,
Kouros without
Spiting the face,
Oh, cog-nos-centi
Get a job!

4.

With this mouth,
I kiss my mother.

With this, I will give her
mouth to mouth.
With this mouth,
I will sing, *The water is wide*
and *She'll be coming
'round the mountain*
as the candles flicker,
before two strong men
swaddle her in a sheet.
With this mouth,
I say *never, always,*
and *from now on.*
Yes, with this mouth.

5.

Da capo …
Long ago
losing your head
was like losing face.
You were hysterical
(no loss of uterus, though)
out of control
unless you had
the presence of mind
to pick it up,
(here's your head,
what's your hurry?)
carry it, angels
serenading you
like tiny bloated
mariachis
as you walked
to the highest
hill in Paris,
preaching all the way

to become
the patron saint
of headaches.

An Egg's Tale

Social climber,
they called me.
How could I not
when the wall afforded
such a view.
Up there,
I was my own
meeting. But the higher,
the harder, and like a top
without spin,
I fell.

Mother always said
there's no failure
in it. Success
is getting up again.
She would have wept
to see me: scattered
white lies, a viscous
pool of self-pity,
all the horses,
and the secret service
in sunglasses, shaking
their earpieces until finally
the king showed up,
a flash of gold-buckled
loafer emerging
from the bulletproof black
to kneel where I lay.

To my relief,
he did not speak
of honor or omelets
but scooped me up,

cradled my yellow heart
still unbroken in his palm
and gently swirled me round
like bourbon in a tumbler.
They say keep your friends close
and your enemies closer,
so when he lifted me
to his mouth I knew
I had arrived at last.

As After a Sleep

*Look at the death rate in Alaska
and the death rate in Florida.
If you were old, would you move
to Florida?* asks the biostatistics
professor. All those moves
away from family, languages
just learned, jobs barely
mastered, away from the broken,
hard to fix, only to find myself,
not in Florida, but a place like it,
in the city where I was born,
the city my mother has never left,
six blocks from her dark apartment,
twelve feet wide, four miles from
the tidal basin she rode around
on the roof of a limousine at eighteen,
mink stole over her shoulders, tiara
in her hair, past cotton candy trees,
waving Cherry Blossom Princess 1954.

In a month, the trees the Japanese
gave in 1912 will bloom again
as every year. *Resurgence: a rising again
into life, activity or prominence,* as after
dormancy, remission, as after a sleep
we knew we would wake from.
We will promenade beneath them,
pilgrims circumambulating the water,
my mother pale and curled
in her wheelchair as it glides over
the fallen flowers, her face
turned upward, eyes closed
to the pink-white reaching.

Taking a Bow

She is holding court in bed, wearing a pajama top
and diaper. She did not turn away these visitors
bearing Malbec, who crossed the country to see her,

much as she might have wanted. Many days
when her best friend phones, she eyes caller ID,
lets it ring. Steroids have plumped her cheeks,

but her legs, right ankle resting on bent left knee,
are wire hangers. She is eating, almost supine
("it worked for the Romans"), soft French cheese

with her fingers. Arm outstretched, she sweeps
her wine glass from right to left as if to redirect
applause offstage to someone more deserving

and declaims, "I'm in the arms of Morpheus."

In the Arms of Morpheus I

She rises from the commode,
pull-ups at her ankles, then dizzy,
falls forward, forearms, palms
on the bed. She shakes her head,
sighs *singerie,* French for monkey
business. She doesn't want

a spanking, only to say
in
as
few
as
possible
what she sees when she sees
herself this way—Rococo ape
posturing in brocade, prehensile
tail peeking out, signing:

mannered	irreverent
neither erect	nor on all fours
corseted	extruding

Pussy's in the Well

The town bell tolls.
Two mossy moons,
blinkless and full.
Where's Tommy Green?
Looking for thrills.

The church bells ring.
Time for prayer,
a noon hanging
or another dare.
What is mourning?

The bells do chime.
Don't blame Tommy.
Poor motherless child,
lacks empathy.
Give him time.

Sing ding dong hell.
Other people
braking him dull.
What is cripple?
See how they fall.

Wedding bells shout.
Tom's nude bride lies
beneath a shroud.
Her well's run dry—
cover the mouth.

In the Arms of Morpheus II

Others clean and comb.
She has only to eat,
excrete. She feels most
in the driver's seat,
hands at 10:00 and 2:00,
when gripping
the remote control
with one, bottle
of morphine
in the other.
....

It's not enough,
she insists.
A whole unopened bottle
is not enough.
Are you in pain?
No, no, she says,
irritation in her voice.
Not enough
to put an end
to *this*.

There's a fist in poignant
....

Her last dose two days
ago, the black gnats
in each iris turned fat flies,
she doesn't look at me,
only a spot on the ceiling,
a driver reading the road
signs, afraid to miss the exit.

In the Arms of Morpheus III

Ushered past empty velvet
seats to a baritone boudoir
where everything transpires
—oxygen machine overture
gurgling in the pit—
through the wrong end
of an opera glass

in a distant spotlight.

An ebony bed, a cave
burning with flowers,
the wilted elm where dreams
                            hang

golden pupa.

Damasked servants smelling
of dead leaves and wind,
every utterance in super titles
a silent libretto.

Four and Twenty Blackbirds

Cut the crust
Spare the wing
Black steam
Trilling free

Serve a slice
Savor mince
Beak bites
Rake the throat

Coughing king
Talons grip
Fur squirm
Breath of mouse

Ermine quill
Floating drops
Plucked nape
Subjects see

Royal lids
Hatch new eyes
Still born
Yellow beads

Flaccid neck
Clatter crown
King down
Empty nest

Falling up
Six pence dirge
Strange pie
Sovereign sky

Merry-Go-Round

We are waiting in line for the carousel. My mother's breath is short and shallow. The closer we get, the more I must support her. *I'm dizzy,* she says. *I have to lie down.* Her breath as if. In labor. When the man opens the gate, takes our ticket, everyone runs past, scrambling for a horse. Like a game of musical chairs, no one wants to be left standing in the lights, the mirrors, and organ music. I fall into an empty horse-drawn carriage that no one wants, cradling my mother, weightless and soft as a withered peach. She is naked except for a towel. Her legs across my lap, we are a pietà after the bath. No diaper, no oxygen, no false teeth, no, no, and we begin to turn. *There is the Capitol,* everyone cries. *There is the Castle, the Washington Monument, the Natural History Museum.* The horses jump invisible hurdles while we remain on the ground, going round. A few more turns and my mother is humming softly. Her *life is but a dream* ends and my *row, row, row your boat* begins, and we are a double helix gentling down the stream. The carousel is winding her backwards, from gray-cropped hair to a red braid. Gathering her into my arms, I stand up, steady on the spinning platform, and carry her to the palomino pulling us. I place her on it and wrap her hands around the pole. She does not look at me, not at the Capitol, not at the Castle, not at the Monument, not at the Museum. The steeds on either side, merrily all around, gallop up and down, but my mother's horse glides up, up, up. She is holding on, rising above the others, stirruped Mary Janes out of reach, her horse's blue mane rippling like a hoisted flag. No one can hear me shouting, *Stop! Stop the carousel!* My mother's head is about to touch the canopy, which I see now isn't a painting of clouds.

Acknowledgments

Thank you to the editors of the following publications in which these poems originally appeared:

Alaska Quarterly Review: "Grammar School"

CHEST, American College of Chest Physicians: "I Regret to Inform You"; "Returns & Exchanges"

Cimarron Review: "A Perfect Sacrifice (still it lingered near)"

DMQ Review: "The Night Kitchen"

Fairy Tale Review: "Jack Sprat"; "Four and Twenty Blackbirds"; "Husband Peter"; "The Old Woman in the Shoe"

Gulf Coast: "Merry-Go-Round"

The Ilanot Review: "The Queen of Hearts"

Lunch Ticket: "Dialogue with the Body"

Poet Lore: "Ladybird Ladybird Fly Away Home Your House Is On Fire" (as "Tepoztlán, Mexico")

Sliver of Stone: "In Transit"

www.ingramcontent.com/pod-product-compliance
Lightning Source LLC
Chambersburg PA
CBHW021200080526
44588CB00008B/425